CROCHE

Tunisia...
Baby Blankets™

Designs by Kim Guzman

General Information

Many of the products used in this pattern book can be purchased from local craft, fabric and variety stores, or from the Annie's Attic Needlecraft Catalog *(see Customer Service information on page 16).*

Contents

Bobbles & Lace 2

Cotton Candy 4

Houndstooth 6

Princess Lace 8

Shadow Diamonds 10

Basket Lace 12

Stitch Guide 15

Bobbles & Lace

SKILL LEVEL

INTERMEDIATE

FINISHED SIZE
41 inches x 45 inches

MATERIALS
❏ TLC Baby fine (sport) weight yarn (6 oz/ 490 yds/170g per skein): 4 skeins #7812 sky blue
❏ Size I/9/5.5mm afghan hook or size needed to obtain gauge
❏ Size G/6/4mm crochet hook or size needed to obtain gauge

2 FINE

GAUGE
Afghan hook: 17 sts and 10 rows in pattern st = 4 inches square

SPECIAL STITCHES
Tunisian knit stitch (tks): Insert hook between front and back vertical bars, coming out at back of work, yo, draw up a lp.

Tunisian double stitch (tds): Yo, insert hook in indicated st as for tks, yo, draw up a lp, yo, draw through 2 lps on hook.

Tunisian bobble stitch (tbs): Tds 4 times in indicated st, yo, draw through 4 lps on hook, ch 1 tightly to secure.

Bobble: Holding back last lp of each st on hook, 3 dc in indicated st or sp, yo, draw through all 4 lps on hook.

Double V-stitch (dV-st): ({Dc, ch 3} twice, dc) in indicated st or sp.

INSTRUCTIONS
AFGHAN
Row 1 (first half): With afghan hook, ch 160, draw up lp in 2nd ch from hook, draw up lp in each rem ch across. *(160 lps on hook)*

Row 1 (2nd half): Yo, draw through 1 lp on hook, [yo, draw through 2 lps on hook] across *(1 lp rem on hook counts as first lp of next row throughout).*

Row 2 (first half): Sk first vertical bar, [**tks** (see Special Stitches) in each of next 3 sts, **tds** (see Special

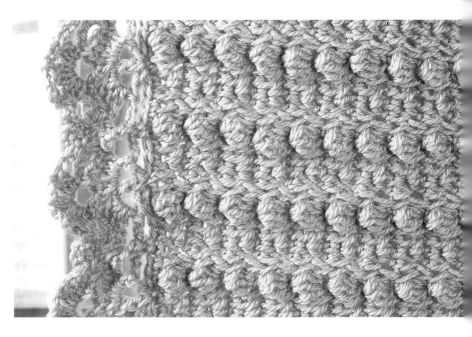

Stitches) in each of next 3 sts] across to last 3 sts, tks in each of last 3 sts. *(160 lps on hook)*

Row 2 (2nd half): Yo, draw through 1 lp on hook, [yo, draw through 2 lps on hook] twice, *ch 1, yo, draw through 4 lps on hook, ch 1, [yo, draw through 2 lps on hook] 3 times, rep from * across until 2 lps rem on hook, yo, draw through 2 lps on hook.

Row 3 (first half): Sk first vertical bar, *tks in next st, **tbs** (see Special Stitches) in next st, tks in next st**, draw up lp in next ch, draw up lp under next horizontal bar at top of row, draw up lp in next ch, rep from * across, ending last rep at **. *(160 lps on hook)*

Row 3 (2nd half): Rep row 1 (2nd half).

[Rep rows 2 and 3 alternately] 52 times. At end of last row, do not fasten off. Remove afghan hook from last lp.

Border
Rnd 1 (RS): With crochet hook, pick up dropped lp, ch 1; inserting hook as for tks, 3 sc in corner sc, 161 sc evenly spaced across last row to next corner, 3 sc in corner; *working over ends of rows across side, 181 sc evenly spaced to next corner*, 3 sc in corner; working across bottom, 161 sc evenly

spaced across, rep from * to *, join with sl st in beg sc. *(696 sc)*

Rnd 2: Sl st in each of next 2 sc, (sl st, ch 1, sc) in next sc, *ch 3, sk 4 sc, **dV-st** (see Special Stitches) in next sc, ch 3, sk 4 sc, sc in next sc, rep from * across to next 3-sc corner group, ch 3, sk first sc of 3-sc group, dV-st in center sc, ch 3, sk last sc of 3-sc group, sc in next sc, rep from * around, ending ch 3, sk last sc of last 3-sc corner group, join with sl st in beg sc.

Rnd 3: Ch 6 (counts as first dc, ch-3), *3 dc in first sp of next dV-st, ch 3, sc in next dc, ch 3, 3 dc in next sp of same dV-st, ch 3**, dc in next sc, rep from * around, ending last rep at **, join with sl st in 3rd ch of beg ch-6.

Rnd 4: Ch 3 (counts as first dc throughout), sk next sp, dc in next dc, *[ch 3, sc in next ch-3 sp] twice, ch 3, sk 2 dc, dc in next dc**, [sk next sp, dc in next dc] twice, rep from * around, ending last rep at **, join with sl st in 3rd ch of beg ch-3.

Rnd 5: (Ch 1, sc, ch 3, sc) in same st as joining, *ch 3, sk next sp ({**bobble**—see Special Stitches, ch 3} twice, bobble) in next sp, ch 3, sk next sp and next dc**, (sc, ch 3, sc) in next dc, rep from * around, ending last rep at **, join with sl st in beg sc. Fasten off. ❏❏

Cotton Candy

SKILL LEVEL

◼◼◼◻
INTERMEDIATE

FINISHED SIZE
39 inches x 45 inches

MATERIALS
- ❑ TLC Baby fine (sport) weight yarn (6 oz/ 490 yds/170g per skein):
  - 2 skeins each #7555 lilac *(A)*, #7812 sky blue *(B)* and #7719 pinkie *(C)*
- ❑ Size I/9/5.5mm afghan hook or size needed to obtain gauge
- ❑ Size G/6/4mm crochet hook or size needed to obtain gauge

2 FINE

GAUGE
Afghan hook: 17 sts and 16 rows in pattern st = 4 inches square

SPECIAL STITCHES
Tunisian knit stitch (tks): Insert hook between front and back vertical bars coming out at back of work, yo, draw up a lp.

Tunisian reverse stitch (trs): Insert hook behind back vertical bar coming out between back and front vertical bars to front of work, yo, draw up a lp.

Shell: ({Dc, ch 1} 4 times, dc) in indicated st or sp.

Beginning shell (beg shell): (Ch 4, {dc, ch 1} 3 times, dc) in indicated st or sp.

PATTERN NOTE
Do not fasten off color not in use. Carry up to working row at beg of each row and pick up as needed.

INSTRUCTIONS
AFGHAN
Row 1 (first half): With afghan hook and A, ch 157, drop A; with B, draw up lp in 2nd ch from hook, draw up lp in each rem ch across, drop B. *(157 lps on hook)*

Row 1 (2nd half): With C, yo, draw through 1 lp on hook, [yo, draw through 2 lps on hook] across to last 2 lps, drop C, yo with A, draw through last 2 lps *(1 lp rem on hook counts as first lp of next row throughout).*

Row 2 (first half): Sk first vertical bar, [**tks** *(see Special Stitches)* in next st, **trs** *(see Special Stitches)* in next st] across, drop A.

Row 2 (2nd half): With B, rep row 1 (2nd half) across to last 2 lps, drop B, yo with C, draw through last 2 lps.

Row 3 (first half): Sk first vertical bar, [trs in next st, tks in next st] across, drop C.

Row 3 (2nd half): With A, rep row 1 (2nd half) across to last 2 lps, drop A, yo with B, draw through last 2 lps.

Row 4 (first half): Sk first vertical bar, [tks in next st, trs in next st] across, drop B.

Row 4 (2nd half): With C, rep row 1 (2nd half) across to last 2 lps, drop C, yo with A, draw through last 2 lps.

Row 5 (first half): Sk first vertical bar, [trs in next st, tks in next st] across, drop A.

Row 5 (2nd half): With B, rep row 1 (2nd half) across to last 2 lps, drop B, yo with C, draw through last 2 lp.

Row 6 (first half): Sk first vertical bar, [tks in next st, trs in next st] across, drop C.

Row 6 (2nd half): With A, rep row 1 (2nd half) across to last 2 lps, drop A, yo with B, draw through last 2 lps.

Row 7 (first half): Sk first vertical

bar, [trs in next st, tks in next s across, drop B.

Row 7 (2nd half): With C, rep row (2nd half) across to last 2 lps, drop C yo with A, draw through last 2 lps.

[Rep rows 2–7 consecutively] 28 time At end of last row, fasten off B and C Remove afghan hook from lp.

Border
Rnd 1: With crochet hook and A, ch 1 3 sc in corner; inserting hook in s across as for row 2 (first half), wor 153 sc evenly spaced across last row t next corner, *3 sc in corner; workin over ends of rows across side, wor 177 sc evenly spaced to next corner* 3 sc in corner; working in sts acros bottom, work 153 sc evenly space across to next corner, rep from * to * join with sl st in beg sc. *(672 sc)*

Rnd 2: (Sl st, **beg shell**—*see Speci Stitches*) in next sc, sk next sc, sc in nex sc, *sk 3 sc, **shell** *(see Special Stitches)* i next sc, sk 3 sc, sc in next sc, rep fron * across to next 3-sc corner group** sk first sc of 3-sc corner group, shell i next sc, sk next sc, sc in next sc, re from * around, ending last rep at **, joi with sl st in 3rd ch of beg ch-4.

Rnd 3: Sl st into first ch-1 sp, ch 1, in same sp, ch 3, [sc in next ch-1 sp ch 3] around, join with sl st in be sc. Fasten off. ❑❑

Houndstooth

FINISHED SIZE
37 inches x 41 inches

MATERIALS

- ❑ TLC Baby fine (sport) weight yarn (6 oz/ 490 yds/170g per skein): 2 skeins each #7624 lime *(A)* and #5011 white *(B)*
- ❑ Size I/9/5.5mm afghan hook or size needed to obtain gauge
- ❑ Size G/6/4mm crochet hook or size needed to obtain gauge

GAUGE
Afghan hook: 17 sts and 14 rows in pattern st = 4 inches square

SPECIAL STITCHES
Tunisian simple stitch (tss): Insert hook from right to left behind front vertical bar, yo, draw up a lp.

Tunisian twisted knit stitch (ttks): Insert hook from left to right between front and back vertical bars of next st, coming out at back of work, yo, draw up a lp.

Bobble: Holding back last lp of each st on hook, 2 dc in indicated st or sp, yo, draw through all 3 lps on hook.

Beginning bobble (beg bobble): (Ch 2, dc) in indicated st or sp.

V-stitch (V-st): (Dc, ch 1, dc) in indicated st or sp.

Beginning V-stitch (beg V-st): (Ch 4, dc) in indicated st or sp.

PATTERN NOTE
Do not fasten off color not in use. Carry up to working row at beg of each row and pick up as needed.

INSTRUCTIONS
AFGHAN
Row 1 (first half): With afghan hook and A, ch 145, draw up lp in 2nd ch from hook, draw up lp in each rem ch across, drop A. *(145 lps on hook)*

Row 1 (2nd half): With B, yo, draw through 1 lp on hook, [yo, draw through 2 lps on hook] across until 1 lp remains on hook *(1 lp rem on hook counts as first lp of next row throughout).*

Row 2 (first half): Sk first vertical bar, [**tss** *(see Special Stitches)* in next st, **ttks** *(see Special Stitches)* in next st] across, drop B.

Row 2 (2nd half): With A, rep row 1 (2nd half).

Row 3 (first half): Sk first vertical bar, [ttks in next st, tss in next st] across, drop A.

Row 3 (2nd half): With B, rep row 1 (2nd half)

[Rep rows 2 and 3 alternately] 76 times, then rep row 2 once. Fasten off B. Remove afghan hook from lp.

Border
Rnd 1: With crochet hook, pick up A, ch 1, 3 sc in corner; inserting hook in sts as for row 3 (first half), work 143 sc evenly spaced across to next corner, *3 sc in corner; working over ends of rows across side, work 167 sc evenly spaced to next corner*, 3 sc in corner; working in sts across bottom, work 143 sc evenly spaced across to next corner, rep from * to *, join with sl st in beg sc. *(632 sc)*

Rnd 2: (Sl st, ch 1, 3 sc) in next sc, *sc in each sc across to next corner sc**, 3 sc in corner sc, rep from * around, ending last rep at **, join with sl s in beg sc. *(640 sc)*

Rnd 3: (Sl st, **beg V-st**—*see Special Stitches*) in next sc, ch 1, dc in next sc *[ch 1, sk next sc, dc in next sc] across to first sc of next 3-sc corner group ch 1**, **V-st** *(see Special Stitches)* i center sc, ch 1, dc in next sc, rep from * around, ending last rep at **, join with sl st in 3rd ch of beg ch-4.

Rnd 4: Ch 3 *(counts as first dc)*, dc i next sp, dc in next dc, *sk next sp (**bobble**—*see Special Stitches*, ch 5 bobble) in next sp, sk next sp**, d in next dc, dc in next sp, dc in nex dc, rep from * around, ending las rep at **, join with sl st in 3rd ch o beg ch-3.

Rnd 5: Ch 1, sc in same st as joining *ch 3, sk next dc, sc in next dc, c 3, (sc, ch 3, sc) in ch-5 sp, ch 3** sc in next dc, rep from * around ending last rep at **, join with sl s in beg sc.

Rnd 6: (Sl st, **beg bobble**—*see Specia Stitches*, {ch 3, bobble} twice) i next ch-3 sp, *ch 3, sk next sp, sc i next sp, ch 3, sk next sp**, ({bobble ch 3} twice, bobble) in next sp rep from * around, ending last rep at **, join with sl st in beg bobble Fasten off. ❑❑

Princess Lace

SKILL LEVEL
◼◼◼▢
INTERMEDIATE

FINISHED SIZE
41 inches x 47 inches

MATERIALS
- ❑ TLC Baby fine (sport) weight yarn (6 oz/ 490 yds/170g per skein): 4 skeins #7555 lilac

2 FINE

- ❑ Size I/9/5.5mm afghan hook or size needed to obtain gauge
- ❑ Size G/6/4mm crochet hook or size needed to obtain gauge

GAUGE
Afghan hook: 17 sts and 11 rows in pattern st = 4 inches square

SPECIAL STITCHES
Tunisian knit stitch (tks): Insert hook between front and back vertical bars coming out at back of work, yo, draw up a lp.

Tunisian double stitch (tds): Yo, insert hook in indicated st as for tks, yo, draw up a lp, yo, draw through 2 lps on hook.

Shell: ({Dc, ch 1} 4 times, dc) in indicated st or sp.

Beginning shell (beg shell): (Ch 4, {dc, ch 1} 3 times, dc) in indicated st or sp.

Cluster (cl): Holding back last lp of each st on hook, dc in each of next 5 dc, yo, draw through all 6 lps on hook.

Beginning cluster (beg cl): Ch 2; holding back last lp of each st on hook, dc in each of next 4 dc, yo, draw through all 5 lps on hook.

INSTRUCTIONS
AFGHAN
Row 1 (first half): With afghan hook, ch 157, draw up lp in 2nd ch from hook, draw up lp in each rem ch across. *(157 lps on hook)*

Row 1 (2nd half): Yo, draw through 1 lp on hook, [yo, draw through 2 lps on hook] across *(1 lp rem on hook counts as first lp of next row).*

Row 2 (first half): Sk first vertical bar,

[**tds** *(see Special Stitches)* in each of next 3 sts, **tks** *(see Special Stitches)* in next st] across.

Row 2 (2nd half): Yo, draw through 1 lp on hook, [ch 1, yo, draw through 4 lps on hook, ch 1, yo, draw through 2 lps on hook] across to last 2 lps, ch 1, yo, draw through 2 lps on hook.

Row 3 (first half): Sk first vertical bar, [draw up lp in next ch, sk next 3-vertical strand group, draw up lp in next ch, tks in next st] across. *(118 lps on hook)*

Row 3 (2nd half): Yo, draw through 1 lp on hook, yo, draw through 2 lps on hook, [ch 1, (yo, draw through 2 lps on hook) 3 times] across to last 3 lps on hook, ch 1, [yo, draw through 2 lps on hook] twice.

Row 4 (first half): Sk first vertical bar, tks in next st, [draw up lp in next ch, tks in each of next 3 sts] across to last ch sp, draw up a lp in next ch, tks in each of next 2 sts. *(157 lps on hook)*

Row 4 (2nd half): Rep row 1 (2nd half).

[Rep rows 2–4 consecutively] 42 times. At end of last row, do not fasten off. Remove afghan hook from lp.

Border
Rnd 1: With crochet hook, pick up dropped lp, ch 1; inserting hook into sts as for tks, 5 sc in corner, work 155 sc evenly sp across last row to next corner, *5 sc in corner; working over ends of rows across side, work 17 sc evenly spaced to next corner*, 5 sc in corner; working in sts across bottom, work 155 sc across to next corner, rep from * to *, join with sl st in beg sc. *(672 sc)*

Rnd 2: Sl st in next sc, (sl st, **beg shell**—*see Special Stitches*) in next sc, *[sk next sc, dc in next sc, ch 1 across to first sc of next 5-sc corner group**, sk next sc, **shell** *(see Special Stitches)* in corner sc, ch 1, rep from * around, ending last rep at **, join with sl st in 3rd ch of beg ch-4.

Rnd 3: Ch 3 *(counts as first dc throughout)*, 4 dc in same st as joining, *[ch 1, dc in next dc, ch 1, 5 dc in next dc] twice, ch 1, sk next dc, dc in next dc, ch 1, sk next dc, [5 dc in next dc, ch 1, sk next dc, dc in next dc, ch 1, sk next dc across to first dc of next corner shell**, 5 dc in first dc of corner shell, rep from * around, ending last rep at **, join with sl st in 3rd ch of beg ch-3.

Rnd 4: Beg cl *(see Special Stitches)*, *ch 3, dc in next dc, ch 3**, **cl** *(see Special Stitches)*, rep from * around, ending last rep at **, join with sl st in beg cl.

Rnd 5: Ch 5, sl st in same st as joining, *3 sc in next sp, sc in next dc, 3 sc in next sp**, (sl st, ch 5, sl st) in next cl, rep from * around, ending last rep at **, join with sl st in beg sl st. Fasten off. ❑❑

Shadow Diamonds

SKILL LEVEL

INTERMEDIATE

FINISHED SIZE
38 inches x 44 inches

MATERIALS
- ❑ TLC Baby fine (sport) weight yarn (6 oz/ 490 yds/170g per skein): 4 skeins #5322 powder yellow
- ❑ Size I/9/5.5mm afghan hook or size needed to obtain gauge
- ❑ Size G/6/4mm crochet hook or size needed to obtain gauge

GAUGE
Afghan hook: 17 sts and 15 rows in pattern st = 4 inches square

SPECIAL STITCHES
Tunisian knit stitch (tks): Insert hook between front and back vertical bars coming out at back of work, yo, draw up a lp.
Tunisian reverse stitch (trs): Insert hook behind back vertical bar coming out between back and front vertical bars to front of work, yo, draw up a lp.

INSTRUCTIONS
AFGHAN
Row 1 (first half): With afghan hook, ch 157, draw up lp in 2nd ch from hook, draw up lp in each rem ch across. *(157 lps on hook)*
Row 1 (2nd half): Yo, draw through 1 lp on hook, [yo, draw through 2 lps on hook] across *(1 lp rem on hook counts as first lp of next row throughout).*
Row 2 (first half): Sk first vertical bar, **trs** *(see Special Stitches)* in each rem st across.
Row 2 (2nd half): Rep row 1 (2nd half).
Row 3 (first half): Sk first vertical bar, [**tks** *(see Special Stitches)* in next st, trs in each of next 13 sts] across to last 2 sts, tks in each of last 2 sts.
Row 3 (2nd half): Rep row 1 (2nd half).
Row 4 (first half): Sk first vertical

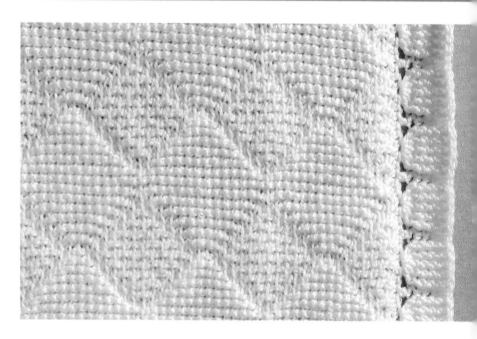

bar, tks in each of next 2 sts, [trs in each of next 11 sts, tks in each of next 3 sts] across.
Row 4 (2nd half): Rep row 1 (2nd half).
Row 5 (first half): Sk first vertical bar, trs in next st, tks in each of next 2 sts, *trs in each of next 9 sts, tks in each of next 2 sts, trs in next st**, tks in each of next 2 sts, rep from * across to last st, ending last rep at **, tks in last st.
Row 5 (2nd half): Rep row 1 (2nd half).
Row 6 (first half): Sk first vertical bar, tks in next st, trs in next st, tks in each of next 2 sts, *trs in each of next 7 sts, tks in each of next 2 sts, trs in next st**, tks in next st, trs in next st, tks in each of next 2 sts, rep from * across to last 2 sts, ending last rep at **, tks in each of last 2 sts.
Row 6 (2nd half): Rep row 1 (2nd half).
Row 7 (first half): Sk first vertical bar, trs in next st, tks in next st, trs in next st, tks in each of next 2 sts, *trs in each of next 5 sts, tks in each of next 2 sts, [trs in next st, tks in next st] twice**, trs in next st, tks in each of next 2 sts, rep from * across, ending last rep at **.
Row 7 (2nd half): Rep row 1 (2nd half).

Row 8 (first half): Sk first vertical bar, [tks in next st, trs in next st] twice, tks in each of next 2 sts, *trs in each of next 3 sts, tks in each of next 2 sts** [trs in next st, tks in next st] 3 times, trs in next st, tks in each of next 2 sts, rep from * across to last 5 sts, ending last rep at **, [trs in next st, tks in next st] twice, tks in last st.
Row 8 (2nd half): Rep row 1 (2nd half).
Row 9 (first half): Sk first vertical bar, [trs in next st, tks in next st] twice, trs in next st, tks in each of next 2 sts, *trs in next st, tks in each of next 2 sts**, [trs in next st, tks in next st] 4 times, trs in next st, tks in each of next 2 sts, rep from * across to last 6 sts, ending last rep at **, [trs in next st, tks in next st] 3 times.
Row 9 (2nd half): Rep row 1 (2nd half).
Row 10 (first half): Rep row 8 (first half).
Row 10 (2nd half): Rep row 8 (2nd half).
Row 11 (first half): Rep row 7 (first half).
Row 11 (2nd half): Rep row 7 (2nd half).
Row 12 (first half): Rep row 6 (first half).
Row 12 (2nd half): Rep row 6 (2nd half).

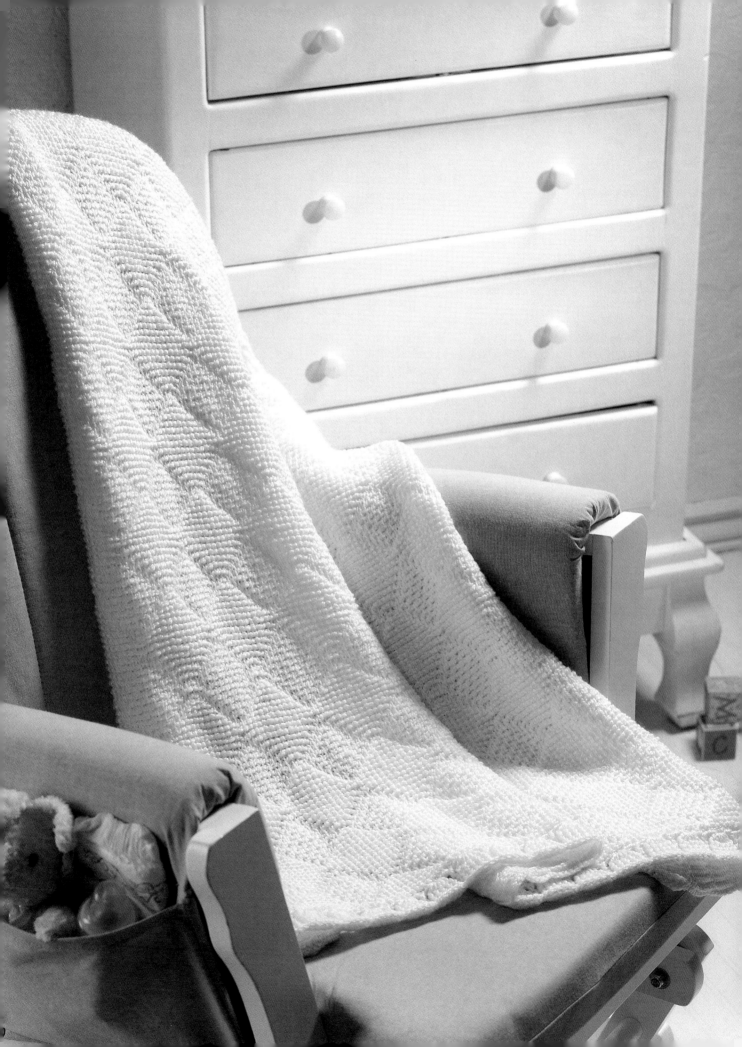

Row 13 (first half): Rep row 5 (first half).

Row 13 (2nd half): Rep row 5 (2nd half).

Row 14 (first half): Rep row 4 (first half).

Row 14 (2nd half): Rep row 4 (2nd half).

Row 15 (first half): Rep row 3 (first half)

Row 15 (2nd half): Rep row 3 (2nd half).

Row 16 (first half): Rep row 2 (first half).

Row 16 (2nd half): Rep row 2 (2nd half).

[Rep rows 2–16 consecutively] 10 times, then rep rows 2–15. At end of last row, do not fasten off. Remove afghan hook from lp.

Border

Rnd 1: With crochet hook, pick up dropped lp, ch 1; inserting hook into sts as for tks, work 3 sc in corner, 155 sc evenly spaced across last row to next corner, *3 sc in corner; working over end sts of rows across side, work 173 sc evenly spaced to next corner*, 3 sc in corner; working across bottom, work 155 sc evenly spaced across to next corner, rep from * to *, join with sl st in beg sc. *(668 sc)*

Rnd 2: Ch 3 *(counts as first dc throughout)*, 5 dc in next sc, dc in next sc, *sk 2 sc, 5 dc in next sc, sk 2 sc**, dc in next sc, rep from * across to first sc of next 3-sc corner group, 5 dc in corner sc, dc in next sc, rep from * around, ending last rep at **, join with sl st in 3rd ch of beg ch-3.

Rnd 3: Ch 1, sc in same st as joining, *fpdc *(see Stitch Guide)* over each of next 5 dc**, sc in next dc, rep from * around, ending last rep at **, join with sl st in beg sc.

Rnd 4: Ch 1, 2 sc in same sc as joining, fpdc over each of next 5 fpdc, 2 sc in next sc, *fpdc over each of next 5 dc, [sc in next dc, fpdc over each of next 5 dc] across to first sc before next corner 5-dc group**, 2 sc in sc before 5-dc corner group, fpdc over each of next 5-dc of corner 5-dc group, 2 sc in next sc, rep from * around, ending last rep at **, join with sl st in beg sc.

Rnd 5: Ch 1, 2 sc in same sc as joining, 2 sc in next sc, *fpdc over each of next 5 fpdc, 2 sc in each of next 2 sc, fpdc over each of next 5 fpdc, [sc in next sc, fpdc over each of next 5 fpdc] across to 2 sc before next 5-fpdc corner group**, 2 sc in each of next 2 sc, rep from * around, ending last rep at **, join with sl st in beg sc.

Rnd 6: Ch 1, sc in same sc as joining, sc in each of next 3 sc, *fpdc over each of next 5 fpdc, sc in each of next 4 sc, fpdc over each of next 5 fpdc, [sc in next sc, fpdc over each of next 5 fpdc] across to 4 sc before next 5-fpdc corner group**, sc in each of next 4 sc, rep from * around, ending last rep at **, join with sl st in beg sc. Fasten off. ❑❑

Basket Lace

SKILL LEVEL

INTERMEDIATE

FINISHED SIZE
36 inches x 42 inches

MATERIALS
- ❑ TLC Baby fine (sport) weight yarn (6 oz/ 490 yds/170g per skein): 3 skeins #7719 pinkie
- ❑ Size I/9/5.5mm afghan hook or size needed to obtain gauge
- ❑ Size G/6/4mm crochet hook or size needed to obtain gauge

GAUGE
Afghan hook: 19 sts and 12 rows in pattern st = 4 inches square

SPECIAL STITCHES
Tunisian knit stitch (tks): Insert hook between front and back vertical bars coming out at back of work, yo, draw up a lp.

Tunisian reverse stitch (trs): Insert hook behind back vertical bar coming out between back and front vertical bars to front of work, yo, draw up a lp.

INSTRUCTIONS
AFGHAN
Row 1 (first half): With afghan hook, ch 154, draw up lp in 2nd ch from hook, draw up lp in each rem ch across. *(154 lps on hook)*

Row 1 (2nd half): Yo, draw through 1 lp on hook, [yo, draw through 2 lps on hook] 8 times, *ch 1, [yo, draw through 4 lps on hook, ch 2] twice, yo, draw through 4 lps on hook, ch 1, [yo, draw through 2 lps on hook] 9 times, rep from * across to last 2 lps, yo, draw through 2 lps *(1 lp rem on hook counts as first lp of next row throughout)*.

Row 2 (first half): Sk first vertical bar, **[tks *(see Special Stitches)* in next st, trs *(see Special Stitches)* in next st] 4 times, tks in next st, draw up a lp in next ch, *insert hook behind front bars of next 3-vertical-bar group, yo, draw up a lp*, [draw up a lp in each of next 2 chs, rep from * to *] twice, draw up a lp in next ch, rep from ** to last 9 sts, [tks in next st, trs in next st] 4 times, tks in last st. *(154 lps)*

Row 2 (2nd half): Rep row 1 (2nd half).

Row 3 (first half): Sk first vertical bar, **[trs in next st, tks in next st] 4 times, trs in next st, draw up a lp in next ch, *insert hook behind front bars of next 3-vertical-bar group, yo, draw up a lp*, [draw up a lp in each of next 2 chs, rep from * to *] twice, draw up a lp in next ch, rep from ** across to last 9 sts, [trs in next st, tks in next st] 4 times, trs in last st.

Row 3 (2nd half): Rep row 1 (first half).

Row 4 (first half): Rep row 2 (first half).

Row 4 (2nd half): Rep row 2 (2nd half)

Row 5 (first half): Rep row 3 (first half).

Row 5 (2nd half): Rep row 3 (2nd half).

Row 6 (first half): Rep row 2 (first half).

Row 6 (2nd half): Rep row 2 (2nd half).

Row 7 (first half): Sk first vertical bar, **[trs in next st, tks in next st] 4 times, trs in next st, draw up a lp in next ch, *insert hook behind front bars of next 3-vertical-bar group, yo, draw up a lp*, [draw up a lp in each of next 2 chs, rep from * to *] twice, draw up a lp in next ch, rep from ** across to last 9 sts, [trs in next st, tks in next st] 4 times, trs in next st.

Row 7 (2nd half): Yo, draw through 1 lp on hook, yo, draw through 3 lps on hook, [ch 2, yo, draw through 4 lps on hook] twice, ch 1, *[yo, draw through 2 lps on hook] 9 times, ch 1, [yo, draw through 4 lps on hook, ch 2] twice, yo, draw through 4 lps on hook, ch 1, rep from * across to last 2 lps, yo, draw through 2 lps on hook.

Row 8 (first half): Sk first vertical bar, **draw up lp in next ch, *insert hook behind front bars of next 3-vertical-bar group, yo, draw up a lp*, [draw up lp in each of next 2 chs, rep from * to *] twice, draw up lp in next ch, [tks in next st, trs in next st] 4 times, tks in next st, rep from ** across to last three 3-vertical-bar groups, draw up lp in next ch, rep from * to *, [draw up lp in each of next 2 chs, rep from * to *] twice, draw up lp in last st.

Row 8 (2nd half): Rep row 7 (2nd half).

Row 9 (first half): Sk first vertical bar, **draw up lp in next ch, *insert hook behind front bars of next 3-vertical-bar group, yo, draw up a lp*, [draw up lp in each of next 2 chs, rep from * to *] twice, draw up lp in next ch, [trs in next st, tks in next st] 4 times, trs in next st, rep from ** across to last three 3-vertical-bar groups, draw up lp in next ch, rep from * to *, [pull up lp in each of next 2 chs, rep from * to *] twice, draw up lp in first st.

Row 9 (2nd half): Rep row 7 (2nd half).

Row 10 (first half): Rep row 8 (first half).

Row 10 (2nd half): Rep row 8 (2nd half).

Row 11 (first half): Rep row 9 (first half).

Row 11 (2nd half): Rep row 9 (2nd half).

Row 12 (first half): Rep row 8 (first half).

Row 12 (2nd half): Rep row 8 (2nd half).

Row 13 (first half): Rep row 9 (first half).

Row 13 (2nd half): Rep row 1 (2nd half).

[Rep rows 2–13 consecutively] 9 times then rep rows 2–6. At end of last row do not fasten off. Remove afghan hook from lp.

BORDER
Rnd 1 (RS): With crochet hook, pick up dropped lp, ch 1; inserting hook into sts as for row 2 first half, work 3 sc in corner, 147 sc evenly spaced across last row, 3 sc in next corner; *working over ends of rows across side, work 163 sc evenly spaced*, 3 sc in next corner; working across bottom, work 147 sc evenly spaced to next corner, 3 sc in corner, rep from * to *, join with sl st in beg sc. *(632 sc)*

Rnd 2: (Sl st, ch 1, sc, ch 3, sc) in next sc, *ch 3, [sk next sc, sc in next sc, ch 3] across to next corner sc**, (sc, ch 3, sc) in corner sc, rep from * around ending last rep at **, join with sl st in beg sc. *(320 ch-3 sps)*

Rnd 3: (Sl st, ch 3—*counts as first dc throughout*, 5 dc) in first sp, *sc in next sp, [ch 3, sc in next sp] twice**, 3 dc in next sp, rep from * across to next corner sp, ending last rep at **, 6 dc in corner sp, rep from * around, ending last rep at **, join with sl st in 3rd ch of beg ch-3.

Rnd 4: Ch 3, dc in same st as joining, 2 dc in each of next 5 dc, *sc in next sp, ch 3, sc in next sp**, 2 dc in each of next 3 dc, rep from * across to next 6-dc corner group, ending last rep at **, 2 dc in each of next 6 dc, rep from * around, ending last rep at **, join with sl st in 3rd ch of beg ch-3.

Rnd 5: Ch 4 *(counts as first dc, ch-1)*, [dc in next dc, ch 1] 10 times, dc in next dc, *sc in next sp**, [dc in next dc, ch 1] 5 times, dc in next dc, rep from * across to next 12-dc corner group, ending last rep at **, dc in next dc, [ch 1, dc in next dc] 11 times, rep from * around, ending last rep at **, join with sl st in 3rd ch of beg ch-4. Fasten off. ❑❑

Stitch Guide

ABBREVIATIONS

beg	begin/beginning
bpdc	back post double crochet
bpsc	back post single crochet
bptr	back post treble crochet
CC	contrasting color
ch	chain stitch
ch-	refers to chain or space previously made (i.e. ch-1 space)
ch sp	chain space
cl	cluster
cm	centimeter(s)
dc	double crochet
dec	decrease/decreases/decreasing
dtr	double treble crochet
fpdc	front post double crochet
fpsc	front post single crochet
fptr	front post treble crochet
g	gram(s)
hdc	half double crochet
inc	increase/increases/increasing
lp(s)	loop(s)
MC	main color
mm	millimeter(s)
oz	ounce(s)
pc	popcorn
rem	remain/remaining
rep	repeat(s)
rnd(s)	round(s)
RS	right side
sc	single crochet
sk	skip(ped)
sl st	slip stitch
sp(s)	space(s)
st(s)	stitch(es)
tog	together
tr	treble crochet
trtr	triple treble
WS	wrong side
yd(s)	yard(s)
yo	yarn over

Chain—ch: Yo, pull through lp on hook.

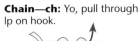

Slip stitch—sl st: Insert hook in st, yo, pull through both lps on hook.

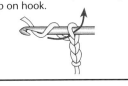

Single crochet—sc: Insert hook in st, yo, pull through st, yo, pull through both lps on hook.

Front loop—front lp
Back loop—back lp

Front Loop   Back Loop

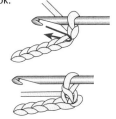

Front post stitch—fp:
Back post stitch—bp: When working post st, insert hook from right to left around post st on previous row.

Back   Front

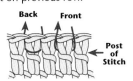

Post of Stitch

Half double crochet—hdc: Yo, insert hook in st, yo, pull through st, yo, pull through all 3 lps on hook.

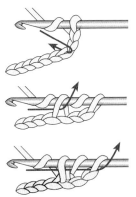

Double crochet—dc: Yo, insert hook in st, yo, pull through st, [yo, pull through 2 lps] twice.

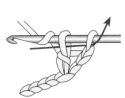

Change colors: Drop first color; with 2nd color, pull through last 2 lps of st.

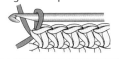

Treble crochet—tr: Yo 2 times, insert hook in st, yo, pull through st, [yo, pull through 2 lps] 3 times.

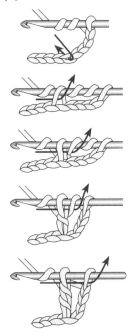

Double treble crochet—dtr: Yo 3 times, insert hook in st, yo, pull through st, [yo, pull through 2 lps] 4 times.

Single crochet decrease (sc dec): (Insert hook, yo, draw up a lp) in each of the sts indicated, yo, draw through all lps on hook.

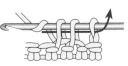

Example of 2-sc dec

Half double crochet decrease (hdc dec): (Yo, insert hook, yo, draw lp through) in each of the sts indicated, yo, draw through all lps on hook.

Example of 2-hdc dec

Double crochet decrease (dc dec): (Yo, insert hook, yo, draw lp through, yo, draw through 2 lps on hook) in each of the sts indicated, yo, draw through all lps on hook.

Example of 2-dc dec

US		UK
sl st (slip stitch)	=	sc (single crochet)
sc (single crochet)	=	dc (double crochet)
hdc (half double crochet)	=	htr (half treble crochet)
dc (double crochet)	=	tr (treble crochet)
tr (treble crochet)	=	dtr (double treble crochet)
dtr (double treble crochet)	=	ttr (triple treble crochet)
skip	=	miss

For more complete information, visit

AnniesAttic.com

306 East Parr Road
Berne, IN 46711
© 2006 Annie's Attic

TOLL-FREE ORDER LINE or to request a free catalog (800) LV-ANNIE (800) 582-6643
Customer Service (800) AT-ANNIE (800) 282-6643, **Fax** (800) 882-6643
Visit www.anniesatticcatalog.com

ISBN-10: 1-59635-123-3   ISBN-13: 978-1-59635-123-3

Printed in USA   1 2 3 4 5 6 7 8 9